D0050079

ANA CASTILLO

My Father Was a Toltec

Ana Castillo is the author of the novels *Peel My Love Like an Onion*, *So Far from God*, *The Mixquiahuala Letters*, and *Sapogonia*. She has written a story collection, *Loverboys*; the critical study *Massacre of the Dreamers*; the poetry collection *I Ask the Impossible*; and the children's book *My Daughter, My Son, the Eagle, the Dove*. She is the editor of the anthology *Goddess of the Americas: Writings on the Virgin of Guadalupe*, available from Vintage Español (*La diosa de las Américas*). Castillo has been the recipient of numerous awards, including the American Book Award, a Carl Sandburg Award, a Mountains and Plains Booksellers Award, and two fellowships from the National Endowment for the Arts. She lives in Chicago with her son, Marcel. Find out more about Castillo at her home-page: www.anacastillo.com.

MY FATHER WAS A TOLTEC

ANA CASTILLO

My Father Was a Toltec and Selected Poems 1973–1988

Anchor Books
A DIVISION OF RANDOM HOUSE, INC.
NEW YORK

FIRST ANCHOR BOOKS EDITION, APRIL 2004

Copyright © 1995 by Ana Castillo
Preface copyright © 2004 by Ana Castillo

All rights reserved under International and Pan-American
Copyright Conventions. Published in the United States by
Anchor Books, a division of Random House, Inc., New York,
and simultaneously in Canada by Random House of Canada
Limited, Toronto. Originally published in hardcover in the
United States by W.W. Norton & Company, Inc., New York,
in 1995.

Anchor Books and colophon are trademarks
of Random House, Inc.

Library of Congress Cataloging-in-Publication Data
Castillo, Ana.
My father was a Toltec and selected poems, 1973–1988 / Ana Castillo.
p. cm.
1. Hispanic Americans—Poetry. 2. Chicago (Ill.)—Poetry.
3. Gangs—Poetry.
I. Title.
ISBN 1-4000-3499-X
PS3553.A8135 M9 2004
811'.54—dc22   2003062897

www.anchorbooks.com

Printed in the United States of America
10 9 8 7 6 5 4 3 2

A los y las Toltecas—
del pasado, presente y porvenir

Contents

Acknowledgments

ALL of *My Father Was a Toltec* (Novato, Calif.: West End Press, 1988) appears here. This revised edition also includes some of the poems from *Women Are Not Roses* (Houston: Arte Publico Press, 1984). There are also selections from *The Invitation* that appeared in a chapbook in two self-printed editions in 1979 and 1986 and from my first chapbook, *Otro Canto* (Chicago: Alternativa Publications, 1977). The five selected poems were first published in the following:

"Juego": *Las Mujeres* (UC–Santa Cruz), 1987.
"Last Sunday": *River Styx* (St. Louis), No. 7, 1980.
"La una y cuarto": *Fem* (Mexico City), 1986.
"Invierno salvaje": *Arizona Canto al Pueblo*, 1980.
"Our Tongue Was Nahuatl": *Revista Chicano-Riqueña*, Año 4, Otoño 1976, Num. 4.

The grammar guard of the Spanish here was Nina Menéndez. (Gracias, gitana, ya sabes—we'll always have Paris!)

I am grateful to all those who have asked for these poems to be made available again and to Gerald Howard and Susan Bergholz for making it possible.

Un saludo de agradecimiento a quienes han estado en la búsqueda de los poemas que finalmente aqui aparecen.

In memory of the Toltec, 1933–1990.

Contents

IN MY COUNTRY

WOMEN ARE NOT ROSES

Contents

Preface

Hark! The Toltecs live! Not the distinguished Mexican people who were already myth at the time of the Conquest, but the Toltecs of Chicago. Imagine my surprise when I moved back to my hometown with my son, ten years after our departure, five years after my father's death, to discover the memory of the Toltecs living on with the survivors of my father's clique. Invariably, whenever I do a public presentation in the city, someone from my baby-boomer generation comes up and tells me her father or uncle was a Toltec from the old neighborhood. The old neighborhood was Taylor Street in the Near West Side of town. Much of it was demolished to make room for the ever-sprawling University of Illinois campus.

For a long time I hated it. On principle.

When I was nearly ten we were among the last families on our block forced to relocate so that our building could be torn down to make room for the dreaded university project. Where our house stood, they put up a parking lot. We were renters and the only help we recieved from the city for our displacement was that someone found an apartment for us a little further up on Taylor Street where I ended up growing into adulthood.

My father was a young dad, nineteen when he married my mother and twenty when I was born. She was a little older and far more mature, so she put up with "the Toltec" for some years before he settled down to a stable family life. The Toltecs were comprised of guys from the neighborhood. They were first generation Americans for the most part and some had come up from Texas. In any case, Mexican was Mexican back then. You settled in the Mexican neighborhood and you married a girl from the neighborhood. You left the neighborhood to work—that was the advantage of Chicago, there was work—but you didn't move too far.

The Toltecs were Mexican just like the first Mayor Daley was Irish. The Irish all lived in a predominantly Irish neighborhood back then. Blacks lived on the South Side—far south. Whites—white Whites—on the north. Jews lived really north and in Hyde Park. You get the picture. You knew exactly what territory you were riding into within the city limits of Chicago just by crossing a viaduct, and had to be prepared if the neighborhood was not friendly to your race or color.

My father was clear that *the Toltecs* were not violent, at least not anywhere near what anyone considers normal gang activity today. They thought they were cool and maybe they were. One of the frayed Kodaks I have with him in a shark-skin suit, holding a cigarette, tall and lean like Nat King Cole, certainly shows evidence of what constituted "cool" in the early sixties. Or the one of him with bongo drums between his rail-thin legs and his friend, *Titi*, still in his Army uniform coming back from Korea, playing maracas. In one of my favorites, the Toltec is bouncing me off his chest. In a T-shirt and duck-tail coming unraveled, he is laughing for the camera, laughing for my mother—the family photographer. I am in diapers and have two teeth growing in. He is ever so cool growing older, posing with suit and tie with Pérez Prado and with Ray Barretto and with Tito Puente who he got to pick up at the airport through the dispensation of another Toltec who had gone into the mambo promotion business in Chicago.

Look up the Toltecs on the Internet or better yet, at your local library where you can sit down with them and read of their inimitable accomplishments. No Aztec worth his salt did not claim lineage to that noble civilization. In my research for another book I discovered something very interesting, a true caveat for a "Chicana feminist" like me. The Toltecs also had queens who ruled. They went out to battle as was the expectation of rulers. It was said that when a certain Queen Xochitl died in battle, her blood ran and spelled out: "This is the end of the Toltecs."

Centuries later, the young Chicago men who took that name used it proudly. They knew, or at least the one who came up with "The Toltecs" did, that they had a heritage to claim. Departing from the Toltecs, however, and the ambition of youth to be brave and defiant, they didn't have much in common with the original Toltecs. But I must add, in many ways, neither did the Aztecs.

So here I am, fifteen years after the first edition of *My Father Was a Toltec* was published by a small press, holding on with some astonishment to how this modest tribute and meditation has spoken to other daughters (and sons) of Toltecs (i.e. descendents of great mythical tribes throughout the world). Their endurance—and mine—keeps me smiling in my heart. I hope our forefathers would be proud to know we claim them.

As for the Toltecs of the mid-twentieth century that hailed from Chicago, yeah, I'll say it: They were cool, real sharp, man. But then again, I've never forgotten that my father was a Toltec.

Ana Castillo
September 21, 2003
Chicago Chapter of the Toltecs

Introduction

My first experience with the kind of writing that so much later I identified as free-form poetry was at nine and a half years old. I had no idea what I was writing or why I was writing it, possessed suddenly to compose from a place so deep within it felt like the voice of an ancestor embedded in a recessive gene. My paternal abuelita had died.

Instead of giving a boy a bloody nose or climbing on the monkey bars or playing tag during recess in the playground at Goodrich School, for a few days immediately following my grandmother's funeral I wrote. My lines were short, roughly whittled saetas of sorrow spun out of the biting late winter of Chicago, my dark cheeks red and raw. I was in the fourth grade. I didn't know then what was motivating me to write these ephemeral, otherworldly messages, the content of which is lost to me.

I remember vividly the yellow pad on which I wrote them, filling page after page until, bound as it was with heavy glue, it automatically became a little book. The pad was small, ugly; the pages, thick and coarse with a cover of grey cardboard, made exclusively for utilitarian purposes—perhaps for keeping quotas—in the factory where my mother worked.

If it hadn't been that my mother got it for me, and at no cost, at the factory, I wouldn't have had a pad on which to give birth to my first poems. Just as if it hadn't been for turn-ins to the blank side of junk mail and dismembering the business mail envelopes and working around the animal blood on butcher paper, I would not have had paper to draw on.

I hadn't cried over my abuelita's death. I'm sure that I was sad, but I didn't cry. Perhaps my dry tears fell as words onto the yellow pad. But if those tears-turned-words were no more than pain finding expression, it went otherwise unnoticed. Since mine was a world relatively unsophisticated about such things, children's emotions were usually not recognized; but then, it was, of course, also that way for the adults. Still, the curandera abuelita would have known what to do: "Give her té de manzanilla, massage her head, let her sleep with you," she might have advised my stoic mother. All my life, the mother knew there was only one thing she had to do for her children, and that was to rise every day at 4:30 a.m. and go to work until the last factory she was employed at closed down to relocate somewhere in Asia long after I was grown and gone from home. But the ancient abuelita who stayed home was gone, forever, and her curandera advice with her.

Abuelita, now among my spirit guides, appears in much of my writing. The first edition of *My Father Was a Toltec* was dedicated to her.

That book was also dedicated to the daughters of Latino men. As a new generation of Latina writers, we had always willingly and consciously made connections with mothers, grandmothers—our feminine inheritance as women—but we had not yet fully identified the masculine within ourselves and how male models contribute to our way of looking and being in the world. It was that idea that served as the initial impetus for the collection.

And although I was visited upon by poetry quite young, I did not at first see myself as a poet. And although I did not see myself as a poet, my first real poems were published when I was twenty-one. My first two collections, however, were printed by my own efforts when I was twenty-four. Briefly, here is why:

IN the early seventies the fires of the Latino Movement burned throughout the Midwest. In Chicago, much of barrio youth was ignited and became caught up in its unprecedented spirit. There were rallies at City Hall and conferences and similar calls for attention to the concerns of the city's large Latino population.

I was attending a girls' secretarial high school. Once I graduated, the hope, given my family and background, was that I could find an office job. Something clean and out of the factory. But instead— because the flames had reached me, licked my ankles and calves and set me ablaze and I now saw myself as not just one more Mexican in the multitude but part of a major historical shift—I started to send myself to school: first to junior college (which was free), and then to a local college on scholarship.

Although I liked to write a bit, my first loves were drawing and painting. However, negative social attitudes toward people of humble origins, as well as the institutional racism and sexism of the university, discouraged me, so that by the time I finished my B.A. I was convinced that I had no talent. I couldn't draw and I had no right to paint. And I did not paint again for the next fifteen years.

By the time I was twenty my creative impulses had been channeled into street-wise poetry. In 1974, I did my first poetry reading. Throughout my twenties, I almost always read with musical accompaniment—from Afro-Latin rhythms to Native American flute to South Side–style jazz to classical and flamenco guitar. The idea of a Chicana poet was scarcely heard of in Chicago. More owl than peacock, I was surprised that I took to the stage with certain ease. Just as with the poetry that came to me as a child and for which I had no name, what I did instinctively in delivering poetry, mine and that of others, was later identified for me as performance art. This unintended appellation notwithstanding, I've never considered myself a performer.

As for the *writing* of poetry, having no models that spoke to my experience and in my languages, I decided that I would never ever take—and never ever have taken—a workshop or a writing class at any time anywhere. I was afraid that I would be told that I had no right to poetry (as I had been told about painting and drawing), and that I didn't write English or Spanish well enough to write. So, while I was indeed intent on being a good poet, I had to carve out for myself the definition of "good."

In my poems I quite consciously addressed my people. But I should add that I was not attempting solely to reflect our concerns but was often writing out of personal experience. And since I was addressing *my* people, I did not feel self-conscious. It felt like talking with familia, something intimate and our own.

These were the circumstances that informed the poems in my first chapbook, *Otro Canto* (1977). Since mine was a collective identity, I used the lowercase "i" in all my early poems as well as in my first novel, *The Mixquiahuala Letters*; and having stated that, I may now put to rest the question most frequently asked of my early writing.

By the late seventies, the great blaze was turning to ashes. And I, too, had "burned out." While a U.S. Latina poet would only rarely have the opportunity to write for major periodicals or publish with a mainstream publisher, she could hope to publish with a small press. For the poet, especially, small presses offer a long-desired trapdoor to the larger world. However, again for Latino/a poets, these avenues were—and are to date—still limited. Thus a few Latino/as across the country began their own publishing imprints. And if even that narrow opportunity to publish was not available, a poet might decide to print her work herself. This is why I "published" my two chapbooks, *Otro Canto* and later *The Invitation*, mostly with the support of friends.

FROM 1973 to 1979 I worked with several Latino artists' groups—all led by men. Often, I was the only woman in the collective. In addition, I was overworked, underpaid (when paid at all), and living a very spartan existence. Consequently I experienced severe "burn-out", which, moreover, I will dare to say may have been due in part to being overexposed to dangerously high doses of testosterone on a daily basis for a few years.

I was crucially aware that departing as a woman from the Latino Movement's goal of seeking retribution on the basis of race, ethnicity, and social status—but *not* on gender—would be a lonely path. Addressing such issues, especially those related to sexuality, was seen as the territory of privileged white women and even interpreted as a betrayal by many Latino activists, both men and women. That was in 1977. It was one of the hardest years of my adult life. All of the important decisions I made at that time were inextricably tied to being a brown, penniless female. And a poet.

At twenty-four, finding myself in retreat in my unheated little basement flat, with not much more than books and a big dog, and all my reflections and assessments about the state of Latinas born in the United States (particularly my own), I turned a sharp focus on writing and women's literature. Being forced to reach that deeply within, almost like the hand of a psychic surgeon, I pulled out all consternation over my recent experiences, feelings that could have turned to rancor, that could have destroyed one more woman rendered inconsequential by society. And I set upon the task—the joyful yet daunting task—of my next project: a small collection of Latina erotica entitled *The Invitation*. In *The Invitation*, I hoped to appropriate our sexuality, our own sense of sensuality, and to invite others to a celebration of self-love.

Still, for a long time, I considered myself not-first-a-poet but a component of the growing Latino artists' community that had begun cutting across borders with machete-like vigor throughout the Americas and Caribbean. I was active not only in Chicago but from 1975 to 1976 also in Northern California and Mexico. The poems "1975" (which was a reflection of the Chicago I had just left behind) and "Napa, California" (written the day I met Cesar Chávez) were composed then, and "A Counter-Revolutionary Proposition" after a stay in Puerto Rico in 1977. The poem "Entre primavera y otoño" was written in New York in 1978, a place I frequented often to join the Latino artists and poets of the Lower East Side. "A November Verse" came after a trip to Brazil, and still later, the poem "For Jean Rhys" (ignored as an artist throughout most of her life) was written in Paris—when Latino/a artists and writers were slashing and burning new frontiers in Europe. In this way our poetics and our artistic movement continued to expand, and in an amorphous way it still exists.

MANY of the poems in *My Father Was a Toltec* (1988) overlap the period of the new poems that appeared in *Women Are Not Roses* (1984). *Women Are Not Roses* included selections from the two chapbooks, *Otro Canto* (1977) and *The Invitation* (1979). I have also sprinkled in five early poems here. All the poems included in this selection are reprints. They were written from the years 1973 to 1988, between the ages of twenty and thirty-four.

Despite all this struggle, despite the social concerns that have given rise to my poems—just as it was in the beginning at the age of nine—for me, writing has always been done in a state of ecstasy. While I may have some idea from where I depart, I cannot know beforehand where I will be until I arrive, and not even then, sometimes, not for a long time. In the end, interpretation is not only the privilege *of* the reader, but a responsibility that belongs *to* the reader.

WITH my poems, I know that I have shot a lot of arrows; but the hand that drew back the bow was always held over my heart.

ANA CASTILLO
February 28, 1994
Tierra de los Seminoles

MY FATHER WAS A TOLTEC

THE TOLTEC

The Toltec

c. 1955

My father was a Toltec.
Everyone knows he was *bad*.
Kicked the Irish-boys-from-Bridgeport's
ass. Once went down to South Chicago
to stick someone
got chased to the hood
running through the gangway
swish of blade in his back
the emblemed jacket split in half.

Next morning, Mami
threw it away.

Electra Currents

Llegué a tu mundo
sin invitación,
sin esperanza
me nombraste por
una canción.

Te fuiste
a emborrachar.

Red Wagons

c. 1958

In grammar school primers
the red wagon
was for children
pulled along
past lawns on a sunny day.
Father drove into
the driveway. "Look,
Father, look!"
Silly Sally pulled Tim
on the red wagon.

Out of school,
the red wagon carried
kerosene cans
to heat the flat.
Father pulled it to the gas
station
when he was home
and if there was money.

If not, children went to bed
in silly coats
silly socks; in the morning
were already dressed
for school.

Saturdays

c. 1968

Because she worked all week
away from home, gone from 5 to 5,
Saturdays she did the laundry,
pulled the wringer machine
to the kitchen sink, and hung
the clothes out on the line.
At night, we took it down and ironed.
Mine were his handkerchiefs and
boxer shorts. She did his work
pants (never worn on the street)
and shirts, pressed the collars
and cuffs, just so—
as he bathed,
donned the tailor-made silk suit
bought on her credit, had her
adjust the tie.

"How do I look?"
"Bien," went on ironing.
That's why he married her, a Mexican
woman, like his mother, not like
they were in Chicago, not like
the one he was going out to meet.

The Suede Coat

c. 1967

Although
Mother would never allow
a girl of fourteen to wear
the things you brought
from where you wouldn't say—
the narrow skirts with high slits
glimpsed the thigh—
they fit your daughter of delicate
hips.
And she wore them on the sly.

To whom did the suede coat with
fur collar belong?
The women in my family
have always been polite
or too ashamed to ask.
You never told, of course,
what we of course knew.

Dirty Mexican

"Dirty Mexican, dirty, dirty Mexican!"
And i said: "i'll kick your ass, Dago bitch!"
tall for my race, strutted right past
black projects,
leather jacket, something sharp
in my pocket
to Pompeii School.
Get those Dago girls with teased-up hair
and Cadillacs,
Mafia-bought clothes,
sucking on summer Italian lemonades.
Boys with Sicilian curls got high
at Sheridan Park, mutilated a prostitute one night.
i scrawled in chalk all over sidewalks
MEXICAN POWER CON/SAFOS
crashed their dances,
get them broads, corner 'em in the bathroom,
in the hallway, and their loudmouthed mamas
calling from the windows: "Roxanne!" "Antoinette!"
And when my height wouldn't do
my mouth called their bluff:
"That's right, honey, I'm Mexican!
Watchu gonna do about it?" Since they didn't
want their hair or lipstick mussed they
shrugged their shoulders 'til distance gave way:
"Dirty Mexican, dirty Mexican bitch."
Made me book back, right up their faces,
"Watchu say?" And it started all over again . . .

For Ray

i found a stash of records
at the Old Town Street Fair.
Gave up Perez Prado,
"Rey del Mambo,"
to Ray.

But Cal Tjader's
Soul Sauce
Guacha Guaro
cooler than
a summer's night breeze—
Della Reese in spaghetti strap
dress cha-cha-cha—
is *mine.*

And who am I?
A kid on the güiro
who no one saw jamming
scrawny and scabby kneed
didn't sing Cucurucucu Paloma
or Cielito Lindo but happy
to mambo
please to teach ya
all of seven then . . .

Now, with timbales
and calloused hands
not from a career of
one night stands but the grave
yard shift on a drill press,
Ray thrills the children

who slide in party shoes
at Grandpa's house where
the music blares and it's
all right guacha guaro
guacha guaro it's all right.
My daddy's still *cool*.

Daddy with Chesterfields in a Rolled Up Sleeve

The school principal was a white lady
who came to class one day
to say a man claiming to be
my father
was in her office.

Later at tío Manuel's flat
Daddy said Mami was
on her way. (*It must be serious,*
i thought, Mami never misses work.)

All Manuel's tribe gathered:
rotten toothed daughters with children
of varying
hair textures and surnames;
Davíd, a junkie,
mean face of an Apache;
Daniel, smiled nice, did nothing
with his life;
Abel and his boy Cain;
Juanita my madrina, the eldest,
never married.
Twelve children my uncle raised,
his wife died with the 13th.

But this guy across the table
is young with acne,
hair greased back. He smokes cigarettes,
doesn't ask permission, speaks English
with a crooked smile: charm personified.
Hangs out with the boys,

who call him Brodock (they all have
names: Ash Can, Monskis, El Conde,
Joe the Boss, Ming)—this man, who Mami says
doesn't like to work,
plays bongos and mambos loud all day
while Abuelita keeps me out the way
of boys jamming, drinking beer,
while wives work the assembly line.

At tío Manuel's where Daddy took me on the bus,
the Spanish radio has announced
the death of Doña Jovita.
The curandera from Guanajuato—
with jars of herbs
grown in coffee cans—
had raised the Toltec long
after her sons had grown,
her only daughter murdered by her husband.
The boy, the story goes,
was brought forth by the curandera,
or, if you please,
Doña Jovita, herself,
gave birth to him at 60.

And Daddy, who never looks at me
and talks to me at the same time
says "Granny died," and begins to cry.
Daddy is the only one
who calls her Granny.

And i, most delicate of her offspring:
Ana María. Ana María learns English in school,
wears gold loop earrings in mother-pierced ears,
brings flowers to the Virgin every spring.

Anita knows yerba buena, yerba santa, epazote,
manzanilla, ruda, addresses spirits
with Abuelita, touches soreness of those
who come, little hands under
shriveled ones, that heal.

"Granny died," he said, and cried.

Daddy's white foreman
who doesn't believe his mother died,
comes to watch Daddy cry at the coffin.

Every year Mami makes enchiladas for Daddy's birthday,
·never as good as the memory of his mother's.
Mami takes her place now,
tells his daughter to her face:
"You're like your father,
don't like to work,
a daydreamer,   .
think someday you'll be rich and famous,
an artist, who wastes her time
travelling,
wearing finery she can't afford,
neglecting her children and her home!"
The father lowers his eyes.

Had i been 19 not 9
i'd have pulled my hair,
screamed her name, "Don't leave!
Don't leave me behind with this mami
who goes off to work before light
leaves me a key, a quarter for lunch,
crackers for breakfast on my pillow
that rats get before i wake!
Don't leave me
with this mami who will empty out all
your jars, the trunks of your defunct
husband's moth-eaten suits,
the Toltec's wind-up toys,
to move bunkbeds into your
room where you stuck crucifixes
with chewing gum on an old iron headboard!
(A testimony to your faith—
yet the Church did not grant you a Mass
upon your death.)
Don't leave me with this daddy,
smooth talkin', marijuana smokin',
mambo dancin', jumpin' jitterbug!"

The only woman who meant anything in his life.

—No creo que fue tu mamá,—your wife whispers.
"I don't care!" you reply.
—Que ni eres mexicano,—
"I don't care!" you say for
doña Jovita,
la madre sagrada

su comal y molcajete,
la revolución de Benito Juárez y Pancho Villa,
Guanajuato, paper cuts, onyx, papier-mâché,
bullfighters' pictures, and Aztec calendars.

i speak English with a crooked smile,
say "man," smoke cigarettes,
drink tequila, grab your eyes that dart
from me to tell you of my
trips to México.
i play down the elegant fingers,
hair that falls over an eye,
the silk dress accentuating breasts—
and fit the street jargon to my full lips,
try to catch those evasive eyes,
tell you of jive artists
where we heard hot salsa
at a local dive.
And so, i exist . . .

At 15,
Mami scorned me for not forgiving you
when she caught you
with your girlfriend. Had i been 25,
i'd have slapped you, walked out the door,
searched for doña Jovita who loved for no reason
than that we were her children.

Men try to catch my eye. i talk to them
of politics, religion, the ghosts i've seen,
the king of timbales, México and Chicago.

And they go away.
But women stay. Women like stories.
They like thin arms around their shoulders,
the smell of perfumed hair,
a flamboyant scarf around the neck
the reassuring voice that confirms their
cynicism about politics, religion and the glorious
history that slaughtered thousands of slaves.

Because of the seductive aroma of mole
in my kitchen, and the mysterious preparation
of herbs, women tolerate *my* cigarette
and cognac breath, unmade bed,
and my inability to keep a budget—
in exchange for a promise,
an exotic trip,
a tango lesson,
an anecdote of the gypsy who stole
me away in Madrid.

Oh Daddy, with the Chesterfields
rolled up in a sleeve,
you got a woman for a son.

LA HEREDERA

Alternatives

yes—yes
we—no
so
maybe i can be
an "exotic" version
of Pati Smith/strike
lewd poses for Fan-Belt
Mag/make heavy comments to
Time like "i'm into Razor Blades,
mon, double edged, of *coarse*"/my shaved
head back up could call itself Los Razor
Blaids and wear shark skinned suits without
collars and very pointed high heeled boots/my
poems would emit musk—and would NEVER be repeated
except by electronic sound and to make it that much
more heavy, mon, i'd muffle the mike with pantyhose so
nobody would know how heavy i really was and up would go
the acoustic guitar to accent the poetry of my ever so heavy
mammary glands and that's how they'd remember me in Paris before
i toured Morocco and sent Japanese adolescents en masse to Spanish
courses in Tokyo figuring i was too heavy to be reciting in Yankee tongue
and Beirut loved me because i wasn't exotic but actually a long lost Lebanese
compatriot and Xmas holidays i'd relax in the Caribbean or Mexico, right off the
coast, of course, where not even the tourists would recognize me, so naturally brown
Indian brown, before the tan and my working class folks back in Chicago would still be
wondering when i was going to settle down to a decent, stable job although the postcards
are nice and the cover picture on *People* was something to save for the relatives in San
Antonio but so blurred it was hard to tell it was really me next to those pelones that
travel with me and are becoming unworthy millionaires off my brains and possible talent
and all this happened shortly before i was taken to a hospital with my wrists intact
since i wasn't really into razor blades but something sawed through a very delicate
place in my head and it split in two precise halves so that i was assigned a very
bland room without doorknobs on the inside and without bars but the windows did
n't open anyway and my mother knew it all along when it was discovered that my
manager ran off and spent all my investments but being the hard but silent
type she said nothing the day i came "home" talking about teaching or go
ing back to the University of Chicago for a PhD but what would i live
off of meanwhile and i remember my long ago ex-husband who would be
married to a truly exotic, non-English-speaking girl who went into
labor when she found i was back and hadn't even needed a visa and
it would be October because autumn is when bones turn yellow and
all things return to what they once were or really never stopped
being.

For No One, Or Perhaps You

i am carnival
annual holiday from
work and tedium
your masquerade
as mythical hero: marbled
Ulysses. i am Sundays
at the matinee
a fifty cent piece
for candy and popcorn
your first party where girls
formed a motif on the opposite
wall, the last dance of your youth
as dawn broke and you went home alone;
the taut seconds before she
turned the corner,
whose mouth was freshly baked bread,
both your faces flushed
with virginity.

i am the one
with whom you play Houndini.

i am Rome
Rio
Paris
the villages of Mexico
the house maids therein,
that certain actress whose
celluloid thighs were magnified
in their perfection.

i am the spy
in the hole of your conscience.

Woman of Marrakech

As if i were Fatima
you have sex with me
and go away,
Fatima who dances
for men, without one
of her own
who has no inheritance
no home, nothing. Fatima,
whose brother comes after her
with a knife. She is shame.
As if i were sex personified
you remember the way to my
city, my street, the house
where you don't dare knock.

Sex is seven hundred hotel
rooms in Paris, one of them
ours and unused.

It has been a month, one
menstrual cycle. i am a
fly stuck to the light, an
hysterical speck on a linen
collar. You have so many
important things to do. i am
Fatima
a woman
sex.

Recordando un disparate

Llamaste. Se me olvidó cuanto antes que
te había olvidado.
Llegaste después. Desde luego se me quitó
el disgusto. Como niños jugamos.
Me traías tu regalo hecho por tus manos:
—Se llama "Disparate".—Sonreí de acuerdo.

Quise besarte y te besé. Era una tarde
(ayer, para ser precisa) cuando el calor
era aún tolerable.

Querías saber por qué no andaba por la playa,
tomando aire y sol en vez de estar vestida
de gitana, escuchando discos y pensando
en poemas nuevos. Y tú tan pálido
sé que tampoco te asoleas . . .

Y cuando iba a tocar otro disco tú
salías del baño peinado y oliendo
a mi jabón.
—Me voy, Madame—dijiste.
—Sí, como es tu costumbre—dije yo.
—Y antes, me crucificas, como es la tuya—
contestaste.
—Siempre traes tus propios clavos y tu cruz.—

Te fuiste. El beso que me quisiste dar
se esfumó en el aire. Me fui a bañar.
Tenía un compromiso a las ocho.

An Ugly Black Dog Named Goya

An ugly black dog named Goya
witnessed through
glass doors
a woman's legs high
on its master's shoulders.
Goya's tongue hung
panting loud.
Her eyes challenged
Goya's, she called out:
—¡Mira ese perro cochino!—
Thrust interrupted,
irate master threw a shoe,
dog ducked, dejected
by a slew of insults.

From a corner
locked in shadows
Goya pretended to sleep.
Early grey winter inhaled
late afternoon,
obscuring this one—
nothing like his mistress
who was pale and thin,
nervous as a bitch,
brought him fresh meat,
said gaily: "Here, Goya, baby!"
and who was afraid
of men
passing joints on the street,
waiting for tenants
to leave

so they could enter
back windows,
the mistress who cried
one night: "You can have
this dump! I'm going back
to Forest Hills!"

She always phones
at dusk just
to see if another woman
is there
but by then,
the master alone
at work with paints,
canvas, color, books,
and Wagner,
has stopped yelling
at the dog named Goya
too grotesque with hybridism
not to be mean,
lets him lie
near his feet
until the heaviness of winter
exhales a semblance
of light
and they both get to sleep.

Encuentros

encuentros
sobre
consomé de pollo
café de olla
cuando
dos países
dos puntos de vista
dos mundos distintos
se enfrentan
cara a cara

                    él a ella
                    ella evita pregunta
                    tras pregunta

empiezan
a quejarse
de tortillas frías
mendigos que paran
a comer con sus
ojos
sin vergüenza
mientras

                    el sol desparace
                    sigue siendo día

"dicen
que en francia
no se bañan"
ella habla
fusilando
un ambiente sin
chiste

              "parece
              que va a llover"
              viene
              la respuesta

Y aún no se les
ocurre preguntar
sus nombres

Mi Comadre me aconseja

Mi comadre me aconseja que te olvide
pero siempre he sido una mujer
que a fuerza deja fermentar sus recuerdos,
como mis 30 años de inviernos,
más impenetrables que la verga del diablo,
y como la madre que me dio
su último beso el día de mi primera comunión,
que fue también
cuando su marido la dejó.

—*Tu padre, tu padre,*
ese hombre, esos hombres,
que no trabajan
que no les importan sus hijos
que no más andan con la bebida
y 'tras de las faldas,
esos hombres—

Y nadie, ni mi comadre sabe
cuánto me gustas

aún más, cuando te hago sufrir.

La Heredera

Soy
de huesos finos
de cabello liso
que se convierte
en hilos dorados
en el verano
soy toda de oro.

En un dedo
el anillo
cuyo brillo atrae
tu mirada
a mi mano,
el cigarillo
a los labios llenos
que forman un beso,
el encendimiento
invita a los ojos
negros
que se cierran
como barreras.

Lamento de Coatlicue

Cierro los ojos
y estás aquí
convertido en noche
Tezcatlipoca,
hijo malcriado.

Después vienen
los cadáveres
a rodearme, y aún
no he abierto
los ojos.

Todo me recuerda tu ausencia

Colgando la ropa
sobre un mecate afuera
de la ventana
la neblina me recuerda tu
ausencia.

En ese piso en Madrid,
se abrían las ventanas así,
como ésta. Todas las vecinas
se empinaban colgando
toallas, sábanas, y calcetines.

En la calle, en el frío
de enero, las manos de las damas
se arrugaban como papier-mâché
mientras fumaban sus cigarillos
y lucían sus pieles de zorro.

Me seguías entonces, como me sigues
ahora, por los museos, como por mi
cocina cuando pongo a cocer
los frijoles, y le sirvo
la leche al niño.

Es por demás.
Tus capacidades de araña me
encuentran en cualquier lugar.
Si me cuelgo yo misma de
un mecate afuera de la ventana,
estoy segura que tu ausencia
me seguirá.

Poem 13

i too
can say
good-bye
effortlessly
silently
remove
myself
from an undesired
space
turn about face
march forward
never
look over
my shoulder
control
memory
erase unnecessary
experience
deromanticize
romance
wind tomorrow
around me
without company
(freeze my womb)
publicize my birth
given name
i too
can be my
mother's child
become my father's
extension

improved upon
gesticulate courage
profess pride
am worth
that much
i too
could live satisfied
with all my acts
content
amidst my ignorance.

For Jean Rhys

1890–1979

Well, hell, shit
sometimes it gets
pretty damn difficult
trying to understand
the human race, don't it?
Exercising language
the species' claim to fame,
instead of just humping
the first being that
goes by.

He talked throughout the night
gave 300 pages
of his unwritten memoir:
the stint
in military school,
narrow escape
from the Jesuits,
the uncle sent to Siberia,
and the present wife,
whom he first loved
in dreams.

She hardly edged in a word
like the last body in the metro
before the train goes off.
She smoked his cigarettes and
drank the bordeaux,
all the while, not losing sight
(in that practical manner

he so obviously detests)
that she was only there
due to circumstances.

At last, calculated sighs, even tears
punctuated with a "Well?"
to heighten the drama.
"Well what?" she replies.
"Well, will you have sex
with me or not?"

Well,
she could have gone to a park
sought asylum in a police station:
"I've been robbed."
100 report forms, the sun up
she'd go out to mix with the crowd.

All she needs is sleep,
in a safe place.
In the morning she'll go out
to mix with the
ruddy faced workers
of nicotine stained teeth
who ride the metro
with a gaze of irradicable
detachment.

She steps out of the bathroom,
powdered cheeks gone limp
like wet clay and leaves,
hardly angry.
Anger was affordable at age 25.
Disillusion long ago an expense.
Now, she has only to find
a place to sleep.

And this morning,
pink dawn above Paris, magenta
where city smog fuses with sky,
she has a café crème on the street
and goes on. No one will notice her
once she mixes with the crowd.
A bag for a pillow,
a coat to keep her warm,
the loud screech of rails,
a subterranean lullaby.

Ixtacihuatl Died in Vain

Ixtacihuatl Died in Vain*

I

Hard are the women of my family,
hard on the mothers who've died on us
and the daughters born to us,
hard on all except sacred husbands
and the blessings of sons.
We are Ixtacihuatls,
sleeping, snowcapped volcanoes
buried alive in myths
princesses with the name of a warrior
on our lips.

II

You, my impossible bride,
at the wedding where our mothers
were not invited,
our fathers, the fourteen
stations of the cross—

You, who are not my bride,
have loved too vast, too wide.
Yet I dare to steal you
from your mother's house.

It is you
I share my son with
to whom I offer up
his palpitating heart

so that you may breathe,
and replenish yourself,
you alone, whom I forgive.

III

Life is long enough
to carry all things
to their necessary end. So
if i am with you
only this while,
or until our hair goes white,
our mothers have died,
children grown,
their children been born,
or when you spy someone
who is me
but with fresh eyes that see
you as Coatlicue once did—
and my heart
shrivels with vanity;
or a man takes me out to dance
and i leave you at the table
ice melting in your glass;
or all the jasmine in the world
has lost its scent,
let us place this born of us
at Ixtacihuatl's grave:
a footnote in the book of myths
sum of our existence—

"Even the greatest truths
contain the tremor of a lie."

*The legend of the twin volcanoes Popocatepetl and Ixtacihuatl in Puebla, Mexico, has it that these were once a warrior and princess of rivaling tribes who came to an end similar to that of the two lovers of Shakespeare's *Romeo and Juliet*.

La Carta

c. 1974

Vea, Ud. he regresado
una vez más
a su hogar,
al que conoció
de niña, corriendo
por las calles mojadas
brincando charcos
ignorando los gritos
de su abuela
y escapando la correa
del abuelo.

Su basílica, Mamá
se está hundiendo,
fue inevitable,
las muchachas usan
el pelo corto y fuman
en la calle,
los hombres . . .
siguen igual.

Todo está muy
moderno
coches por dondequiera
el metro, edificios lujosos
restaurantes elegantes.

Creo, si regresara
le daría mucho orgullo
de ver el desarrollo,
el retorno de una

gloria antigua.
Pero creo, que igualmente
sentiría tristeza, Mamá.
Nada ha cambiado.

Traficante, Too

c. 1971

Dieciocho
casi casi
señorita, pero
padece un dolor
donde no se dice.

El doctor con
dedo de fierro
lo busca.
Anuncia
con gestos gitanos:

—¡No tendrá hijos
nunca! Y si acaso,
será peligroso.
Siguiendo con este
tema, señorita, ¿no
sabe usted que un
hombre no quiere lo
que ya está usa'o?—

En casa le esperaban
madre y hermana.
—Fue sólo empacho—
les contó ella
encerrándose en el
uataclos* donde una
pícara navaja jugó

con las muñecas
hasta la hora
de cenar.

A Sandra que escribió Traficante I

* water closet

Wyoming Crossing Thoughts

i will never
in my life
marry
a Mexican man,
utter
with deep devotion
"Si, mi señor."

i will never
look into his
fervent gaze
compared to the
sunrise.

i can say this,
daughter of one,
sister of another,
mother of a son.
i can say this
and not care.

i will never hold
a Mexican lover
in my arms
tell him
i love him
and mean it.

i won't serve him
a plate of beans
stand by warming
the tortillas
on the comal.

Not i.
Not i.

i will desire him
my own way
give him
what i please
meet him when
and where
no one else sees,

drive an obsidian blade
through his heart,
lick up the blood.

A Marriage of Mutes

In the house
that was his house
where the woman who lived there
cut the vegetables
hacked the chicken
boiled on the stove
and waited across the table
as he ate, with eyes that asked,
Was it all right? Was it enough?—
the woman who slept with him
changed the linen
scrubbed oil from his coveralls
hung laundry on the line
never sought the face of the woman
across the yard who hung sheets,
coveralls and underwear—
in the house where this man lived
so at peace with himself
the air grew sparse one morning.

The hall to the bathroom narrowed
as his feet grew angular and
head lightened.
He startled himself to hear his first
"caw!"—beating black wings against walls,
knocking down picture frames of the woman's
ancestors, the offspring's bronzed shoes
off the buffet.
One could only guess what he might

have said had his beak contained teeth.
The woman who always anticipated
his needs opened a window.

She would have wanted the crow to sit
on the couch
to read with her,
listen to music,
languish in a moment of peace
before the bird who was the man
she had lived with in such gratitude flew off,
but, of course, it was too much to ask.

It had always been too much to ask.

Martes en Toledo

Amanecí sola en Toledo.
Sol contra pared
contra piedra, rechaza todo.

Un viejo nos dijo—maricas—
mientras tomábamos un café
esperando el autobús de las 17.00.
¿Será que no llevabamos los labios
pintaos? Ser americana acaso
te ofendió?

Yo
te había perdonao todo.
Pero esto de llegar a tu vejez
y no ser nada, no Dalí con pesetas
y castillos, admiradores alrededor
del mundo, sino molinero, gerente
del Banco de Bilbao; o tal vez, sólo
un camarero en Madrid—

Sin dientes llegaste a los 60.
Y un juego de ajedrez con Manolo no
alivia esa herida que ha sido
tu vida: lo crudo, lo sangriente,
la guerra, el fallo, la mujer bella
a quien amaste tanto
y quien se hizo vieja nomás
para fastidiarte. Me llamaste
marica. Todo tu odio envuelto
en una palabra.

Tejido de pelo y dientes

Esperándote a ti
me corté
la trenza
con el mismo cuchillo
con que parto
la lengua que hierve
hora tras hora,
apestando los cuartos
y que no como yo
pero que sí le gusta al hombre
con cebollitas en sus tacos.

Esperándote a ti
me quité las faldas y los fondos
con sus encajes y falsas
transparencias.

Por ti
dejé camas desconocidas
para recostarme sobre
la vega de tu cuerpo.
—Ni siguiera tenemos cama—
me has dicho. Contigo no
he llegado a jugar
a las muñecas
vestidas en las crinolinas de Mamá.

Llego madura. Llego limpia,
sencilla, sin mitos
ni misterios.
¿No me lo crees? ¡No me lo crees!
Verás, mi negra dulzura,
mi agridulce blanca. Verás.

Guadalupe

Me faltarías, Guadalupe,
vela que nunca se apaga,
risa de la madrugada
color de la cosecha,
poderosa y llena.

Me faltarías, Guadalupe . . .
tanto esperar
para que llegaras
a dejarme tu alma
envuelto en un costal.

"Mamá" no te digo.
Vale que no eres santa.
Andas por Nueva York
con tu rebaño de gatos,
perros, y niños abandonados.

Tu amor por el cigarro y el vino.
¡Ay! Guadalupe, me faltarías como un destino.
Ya te siento tan lejos
como aquí conmigo.
Te siento por el otro lado
de la luna.
Entre mis venas, atrás de mis pupilas,
profundamente en mis oídos,
donde camino y cuando llamen
tu nombre: yo respondaré

A Lupe Gárnica

Cherry Stained Lips and Thick Thighs

That woman with perfect mouth
stained as if with cherry juice
whom you spied slipping off
red kimono, thick thighs
stepping into afternoon bath
of gardenia essence—
that woman who bore
a child the color Navajo,
went out on Saturday nights,
left you with your books and cigarettes
for Arabian men with money,
a black man who gave her jazz,
and finally settled for the white one
who loved her best
with her thick thighs and fallen breasts
she never let you see
thinking they hung ugly from early
childbearing
"not flawless
like yours," she said,
while you soaked
in your evening bath
with book in hand,
as *she* painted, brushed, sprayed herself
for men whom she demanded at 2 a.m.
they make love to her this way and that.
On the other side of the wall she whispered,
"Down there, I want your tongue down there."

Yet you saw her eyes when
you entered a room, how she caught
her breath. That woman gave you
to her brother one drunken night,
who took you to a hotel.
And as he plunged, your
muted mouth
called her name.

Lunes

mujer cada
díanoche
te acercas

vienes
espero

sabes o no
sabes

tendrás miedo
seré yo eclipse

la tasa de café
frío
entierro la cabeza
entre los brazos
apenas es lunes

¿Dónde Empezar?

Tantas lágrimas, tantas
que llora
y dónde empiezo a acumularlas?
En tinas y cubetas
en ollas de peltre y jarras de barro
se acaban las toallas y las esponjas
el periódico del domingo y mis revistas de moda.

Al fin, mis senos empapados, mi cabello,
mis hombros, las manos que recorren su rostro;
mi boca se abre a tomar su llanto salado.
Tantas lágrimas y en cada gota un cuento
de fracaso.

La casa se hundía y yo nos busqué
una almadía.
Nos fuimos a la deriva adormecidas por la madrugada.
Nos fuimos a la deriva sobre angustias y sueños pesados.
Yo cantándole en murmullos: —Ya no llores, mujer.
Yo no estés triste. Te acabarás llorando.
Ya no llores. Ya, ya, ya . . .

I Am the Daughter/Mother Who Has Learned

i am the daughter/mother
who has learned
devotion,
tenderness,
to mend
the irreparable
and to cultivate.

i know how to labor
with clenched teeth,
to find strength
and gratitude in relief.

But i don't know how
to love.

Does this paper with
printed words without lyric or sound
love?

Does my daughter/mother/lover
believe it so
because i've learned so well
the things i know?

i've learned from conch shells,
prisms, coral,
and granite;
the night without stars,
black pupils of eyes,

dirt embedded in the hard soles
of *guarached* feet.
Politicians, shamans,
and poets call these
mysteries.

The daughter/mother who falls
into bed does not recall love
with practiced gestures
and memorized utterings.

i am the daughter/mother who
cuts the umbilical cord
of umbilical cords
to set us both free.

Released to nowhere,
we can return
to each other
baptized with new names
like nuns sanctified
by virtue of
having named ourselves.

Accusations
of knowing or not,
lessons as
daughters/mothers/lovers
will cease.
If there be

no love even then,
at least
we shall have peace.

IN MY COUNTRY

A Christmas Gift for the President of the United States, Chicano Poets, and a Marxist or Two I've Known in My Time

i've left philosophy to men,
heirs to their classics,
lovers of silk-laden
self-aggrandizing perceptions.
Poetry, too, belongs to them,
which is attributed
to their feminine side,
mystification of nature, and
relentless desire to be divine.

Their poems that come at night
from a memory of a
suckled breast
ring of epitaphs;
verses pretending to speak
to a friend have no other end
than to be recognized.

So these are not poems, i readily admit,
as i grapple with nonexistence,
making scratches with stolen pen.
One word is a splinter of steel
that flings from the drill press
into my father's eye;
that one, embedded in the thumb
of my child's father.
Another word, also steel,
the rolling pin
my grandmother used for the

last tortillas of her life.
Exclamation points—my
departure from the Church at 18!

Simple expressions, these.

Rape is not a poem.
Incest does not rhyme.
Nor the iridescent blue labor
of the placenta that follows
giving birth. These are not thoughts
great books have withstood time for,
so unlike the embellishment of war
or man's melancholy at being
neither earth nor heaven bound.

My verses have no legitimacy.
A white woman inherits
her father's library,
her brother's friends. Privilege
gives language that escapes me.
Past my Nahua eyes
and Spanish surname, English syntax
makes its way to my mouth
with the grace of a clubbed foot.

So it doesn't matter now
how many lines i read,
institutions i attend.
Something inherent resists
the insistence that i don't exist.

i shall read for pleasure,
write for pleasure,
spend countless hours contemplating
shadows changing the room
with the movement of the sun.
i shall make love
and never tell of it.
My legacies are anonymous.
Nothing matters
while one man can yet
lie to the world,
and the world
chooses to believe him.

Everywhere I Go

Preguntan de donde soy,
y no se que responder.
De tanto no tener nada,
no tengo de a donde ser.
—ATAHUALPA YUPANQUI

My new speech is echoed
with the tongue that sounds
of tumbling wooden blocks,
a peculiar conjugation
of consonantls running tlogether.

Everywhere i go
i am asked my origin
as if i bore antennae
or the eye
of the Cyclops.

Somewhere i squat
to plant seeds, dry
animals skins, paint
clay pots with floral dashes
of red and aquamarine,
place a firm hand—
with an incantation
life emerges.

i walk with gold adornments
pierced through my nose,
gems embedded in drilled holes
in my teeth.

i am loved.

And i love, and am not lost,
nor wander.

El sueño

Lucía
mi traje zapoteco
un huipil
rojo
rojo
color de sangre
zapoteca
brillante
alumbrante
del sol
oaxaqueño
más suave
que los pétalos
de la flor
macizo
como los nopales viejos
que adornan
la sierra
dulce
como el maguey
caliente como el
mezcal.

Lucía mi huipil colorado
por las calles
de una ciudad
tan orgullosa
tan fuerte
que no sentí
el primer golpe
del rechazo.

Entre primavera y otoño

La india carga
su bandera sobre
su cara
manchada de sangre
sus cicatrices corren
como las carreteras viejas
de su tierra
y la india no se queja.

Le preguntan por qué
no cuenta
su historia
y ojos húmedos responden
que le cuentan todo
al que quiera oír.

Si acaso abre
su boca
sale la canción
del mar
los ecos del viento
hay volcanes inquietos
en el pecho de la india.

Sus huesos se han hecho
del polvo
de cincuenta mil muertos
el grito doloroso
de ellos
es el silencio
de la india.

Ayer tuvo un hombre
que le hizo sueños
del aire . . .
tuvo sus hombres
la india
pero ahora no tiene
a nadie.

Del mundo es la india
y si la ves
bailando
en vestido de seda
o pidiendo en la calle
no le preguntes el por qué
ni tal razón por su camino.

El destino de la india
es la bandera que carga
sobre su cara quemada
dura de sangre seca
y la india no se queja
no se queja de nada.

*A mí, en el día que cumplí
los 25 años: Nueva York, 1978.*

Zoila López

If i were you, Zoila,
i wouldn't be here
in English class
with the disturbed child
who sits in the back
with the husband
who doesn't work.
i wouldn't laugh, Zoila,
if my first winter up north
were without boots
and the only thing to
warm me was the photograph
of Jorgito dressed as a
little indian in white
pajamas and sandals on
Guadalupe's Day, just before
he was killed by a truck
that carried oranges.

i wouldn't bathe, change
my dress, look for work,
hold a pencil upright
after this summer when
the baby ran a high fever
and the hospital people in
that marbles-in-the-mouth
language said, "It's okay.
Take her home."
You'd thought she'd just
stopped crying when
she died that night.

i would die, if i were you,
Zoila, a million deaths at
the end of each nightmarish day
with its minuscule hopes like
snowflakes that melt on one's
teeth and tongue and taste of
nothing.

Me & Baby

Chicago, c. 1984

It's me, the pregnant Puerto Rican girls, short Mexicans
with braids down to there, and all the babies in the world

waiting for our numbers to be called. At 3 p.m.,
there's an empty chair past Egberto with bad breath

from beer the night before, Marta and her sister with
strollers between them, autistic boy of the twisted cheeks,

and finally, me & baby get a seat. Women divided
from us by desks, type out cereal, milk, juice coupons,

government approved and labeled at the market. A woman
in back complains in Spanish; another wishes she had welfare.

An African with delicate tribal scars along her face
places her little one on my lap while she

goes to the bathroom. The Salvadoreñas, too glum,
having missed a day of work, don't say a word to anyone.

At 4:45 a man on the night shift left the kids with his wife. He
never lifted his eyes. We must have been an ugly sight.

Baby needs solids the doctor at the clinic has said.
i'll speak up when i get my chance. If they ask me for forms,

and doctor's written requests, i'll pound my fists
on those coupon covered desks. At 5 of 5 i kick the wall instead.

The office is officially closed, coupon books put away, clerks
freshen lipstick, nutritionist hangs her smock, her day ended.

And we, of the numbers uncalled, must come back, take a new
number, start again. Clear the entrance. If there are no

empty chairs, please don't block the way. Sorry, ma'am.
We open at 8. We'll see you tomorrow. Best to arrive temprano.

Paco and Rosa

"AS SOON AS THE CHILDREN
ARE OUT OF SCHOOL
I'LL COME," Rosa shouts
over static
from La Barca to Chicago.
"GOOD," says her husband,
hangs up, sighs.

Tonight he won't
shave, slap on Christmas
cologne, press down his hair.
He won't go to the Paraiso Club
with his brother or to the
corner tavern where a man gets
lost in the smell of hairspray
on a woman whose name he'd
rather not know.

Instead, hands behind his head,
he thinks of Rosa
who smells of the children
the meat-packing plant where
she worked between babies,
the summer they met, La Barca
by the sea. Rosa,
who smells of home.

Cold

Cold
is not once
or twice in a life
not from a window
of a fleeting train
glimmer of sun
so white blinding on
an afternoon it must be
heaven, not
a picture postcard with rose
cheeked children on sleds
or a sleigh ride to a distant
house with smoking chimney, not
a crystal paperweight turned
upside down a flurry falls on
a row of little houses and
evergreens.

It is cold
in the city surrounded by
flatland, nothing but silos
to stave off the wind. Mucus
drips from a child's nose
during its rasping sleep.
Rats curl and nest behind
the stove.
Feet lose feeling for weeks.
Joints stiffen, backs create
new places to ache. A constant
quiver inhabits the body.

Windows rattle and call out
demons. The cracked one
covered with cardboard and tape.

Cold
is not nostalgic.

Winter emits no fond memories.
Although you will laugh
only to find teeth ring
sharply with pain.

Tomás De Utrera's First Poem of Spring

Death comes to us every day
in banal greyness. A boy
jumps into the street
a car runs the light . . .
death comes to us. Siren
aflame and bright. I go
on my way.

A familiar bar,
a shot is 50 cents.
I teach English to Haitians
and other immigrants.
The boy on the tar
a repulsive mass like the boil
on my wife's back so bad
she hasn't been to work in 3 days.
Death comes to us in tricky ways.

In Spain, a day was just a day
but the nights! Oh, the nights!
There was Manos de Plata, not even
a Spaniard, makes more money
than any gypsy on the guitar.
*(That boy on the tar,
a black lump, foot quivers, stops.)*

Arturo with pointed beard,
cognac in hand, laughs
to see me. I also laugh.
Death comes . . .
I owe him 3 bucks or maybe

he owes me.
Anyway, the gypsies on Southport
are not like the gypsies of Spain
        always thinking of money
        eyes on your pockets.
Turn me upside down, bastards
of a saintly mother, turn
me upside down
Amerika! América,
        ¿no sabes que mañana no me da miedo?

Arturo tells the bartender
to make it 2 and put
it on the tab.
Violin under his arm
like a bundle of rags.
I'll be drunk before I'm
home, and won't have told
about the boy.

Arturo's son works in
computers. He's proud.
(Not Arturo, his son, I mean.)
Lives in a highrise
with a doorman named Racine.
Racine smiles all the time
with heavy lidded eyes.

        I have two daughters.
One dances flamenco/disco
the other bangs on the piano.

We watch Wonder Woman at 4:00.
The P.T.A. wanted a vote on a
mimeograph machine. I wanted
an uprising of the Guatemalans.
My name is . . .

> (Death comes to us in our sleep
> clenched between our teeth
> caught in the gold fillings)

I never had a son. What
would I tell him anyway? I have
a daughter, *Angela de la Gloria*—
Dance, Angela, baila! Mamá will gather
the silver coins while Papá
beats on the guitar.

I teach English now and
> death comes . . .
but so what?

SO WHAT AMERIKA?
I am a plague! Vermin!
Live on forever!
You can't make me die.

The following morning
in the newspaper, not a scribble.
The Haitians saw nothing.
That corner . . . not so much
as a bloodstain, a witness,
because I didn't see it, not I.

You can't fool me, Death,
you can't fool me. Come, let's
celebrate! Today is your birthday.

We Would Like You to Know

ribe a la mosca como le
perialismo
ERRADA, aka VICTORIA MIRANDA

e
themselves

ot safe,

y,
t the planet
ny continent
same

m
e

We would like you to know
we are not all
docile
nor revolutionaries
but we are all survivors.
We do not all carry
zip guns, hot pistols,
steal cars.
We do know how
to defend ourselves.

We do not all have
slicked-back hair
distasteful apparel
unpolished shoes
although the economy
doesn't allow everyone
a Macy's chargecard.

We do not all pick
lettuce, run
assembly lines, clean
restaurant tables, even
if someone has to do it.

We do not all sneak
under barbed wire or
wade the Rio Grande.

These are the facts.

We would like you to know
we are not all brown.
Genetic history has made
some of us blue eyed as any
German immigrant
and as black as a descendant
of an African slave.
We never claimed to be
a homogeneous race.

We are not all victims,
all loyal to one cause,
all perfect; it is a
psychological dilemma
no one has resolved.

We would like to give
a thousand excuses
as to why we all find
ourselves in a predicament
residents of a controversial
power
how we were all caught
with our pants down
and how petroleum was going
to change all that but
you've heard it all before and
with a wink and a snicker
left us babbling amongst
ourselves.

No sólo el ser chilena

Pablo le
escribe a
—HILD

Home is not a four-walled struc
or the place where those who ca
friends welcome me.
i leave home because where i ar
is where i am most safe
safety being inconsequential, fin
a sea being the same sea throug
fertile ground tasting as sweet on
the doe eyes of any child being
that form in my belly now.
i would apologize for being
less god than animal but natural
this is not my way.
Sometimes, i recall, as if in a dr
face wet, body trembling, how o
raw meat satisfied my appetite.

Someone Told Me

Gracias a la vida que me ha dado tanto
me dió dos luceros que cuando los abro
perfecto distingo, lo negro del blanco
—V.P.

Someone told me the other night,
over flor de caña rum and listening
to her records, that Violeta Parra
killed herself.
She put a gun to her head
at midnight.
All the neighbors came running
at the sound of the report.
It had something to do with economics
and the desertion of her young lover
for a woman half her age. There was
talk of jealous scenes.
Violeta Parra who composed "Gracias
a la vida" killed herself.
Liberals and politicos might be
disappointed in this account. That
she did not die beneath the blows
of rifle butts or by electric shock,
and instead, died the death
of a woman.

Esta mano

¿poemas?
no tengo
poemas
tengo
esta mano que
escribe
a veces
recuerda
acariciar entre
sombras
cada dedo en busca
cada uña cazadora.
¡Pinta! ¡Cuenta! ¡Di algo!
Me ahogas en tu silencio
acércate, mano necia
sí, así, suave sobre mi
rostro, recorre las piernas
también recuerdan
no como tú, tan segura
orgullosa—tiemblan
no les apena rogar, entre
garse humildemente cada
vez más-¿Sabes un secreto?
Ven, con confianza oye—
creo que eres romántica yo
olvido o será que me voy
lejos lejos la ausencia me
libre o si no ese verso sería
de ella—*la otra*
de dedos, piernas, suspiros pesados
y la demás mierda ¡qué va! su cuerpo

un ojo entero vigilando momento tras
momento monumento. su cuerpo que es
su petate, piso, caja, cárcel, casa,
canasta, campo, columpio, costal, co
mal, tamal, topacio, tan tin tan
to que aguantar tendrá que brotar
poemas, llorar poemas, vomitar y orinar poemas
¿poemas?
no tengo
poemas
tengo
esta mano
recuerda

In My Country

This is not my country.
In my country, men
do not play at leaders
women do not play at men
there is no god
crucified to explain
the persistence of cruelty.

In my country
i don't hesitate to sit
alone in the park, to go
to the corner store at night
for my child's milk, to wear
anything that shows my breasts.

In my country
i do not stand for cutbacks,
layoffs, and pay union dues
companies do not close down
to open up again in far-off
places where eating is the
main objective.

In my country
men do not sleep with guns
beneath their pillows. They
do not accept jobs building weapons.
They don't lose their mortgages, pensions,
their faith or their dignity.

In my country
children are not abused
beaten into adulthood
left with sitters who resent them
for the meager salary a single parent
can afford. They do not grow up
to repeat the pattern.

In my country
i did not wait in line for milk
coupons for my baby, get the wrong
prescription at the clinic, was not
forced to give my ethnic origin,
nor died an unnatural death.

In my country, i am not exotic.
i do not have Asian eyes. i
was not raised on a reservation.
i do not go artificially blonde.
The sun that gravitates to my dark
pigmentation is not my enemy.

i do not watch television, entertain
myself at commercial movie houses,
invest in visual art or purchase
literature at grocery stores.

In my country, i do not stand
for the cold because i can't
afford the latest gas hike. i
am not expected to pay taxers
three times over.

This is not my world.
In my world, Mesoamerica
was a magnificent Quetzal,
Africa and its inhabitants
were left alone. Arab women
don't cover their faces or
allow their sexual parts to be
torn out. In my world,
no one is prey.

Death is not a relief.
i don't bet on reincarnation
or heaven, or lose the present
in apathy or oblivion.

i do not escape into my sleep.
Analysts are not made rich by
my discoveries therein. My
mother is not cursed for giving
birth. i am not made ashamed
for being.

In my world, i do not attend
conferences with academicians
who anthropologize my existence
dissect the simplicity of greed
and find the differences created
out of Babel interesting.

In my world
i am a poet
who can rejoice in the coming of
Halley's comet, the wonders
of Machu Picchu, and a sudden kiss.

In my world, i breathe clean air.
i don't anticipate nuclear war.
i speak all languages. i don't
negate aging, listen to myths
to explain my misery or create them.

In my world the poet sang loud
and clear and everyone heard
without recoiling. It was sweet
as harvest, sharp as tin, strong
as the northern wind, and all had
a coat warm enough to bear it.

WOMEN ARE NOT ROSES

Women Are Not Roses

Women have no
beginning
only continual
flows.

Though rivers flow
women are not
rivers.

Women are not
roses
they are not oceans
or stars.

i would like to tell
her this but
i think she
already knows.

An Idyll

now
i   can   tell
of being swept b
y a god a michael
angelo's   david   a
man of such phys
ical   `perfection,
one could not be
lieve him human.
i can tell of lo
sing all logic b
ut it is not the
same as loving w
hat is false the
refore,   cruel   by
virtue of its fa
lseness.   Imagin
e: the   loveline
ss of a statue . .
. but how many bo
nes would it cru
sh, if one dared
to   carry   it   fort
h? how silly, t
o want to run of
f, and live with
it forever, bene
ath its weight—
expect it to app
reciate one's   ap
preciation—to   y

ield, to give—i
lived once, with
a statue, in the
form of a glorio
us satyr in a po
p legend. i ate
with it slept wi
th it made its b
ed in the mornin
g when it disapp
eared . . . i waited
for its return—
each night.

i went on this w
ay for a year or
so. some whispe
red about my mad
ness and i did n
ot care. women
envied me men we
re dulled by h
is light and tha
t gave me pleasu
re.

one day i said: "
get out, leave he
re, now!" (All w
omen have this re
serve of courage,

and common sense)
he would not move
like a giant ston
e (that of course
he was) so i summ
oned the police a
nd they came thre
e men protected b
y badge, gun, and
the law and i saw
. . . his beautifull
y constructed hea
d fall, his beaut
iful blue eyes lo
wer and we stood,
before him in awe
of such beautiful
useless beauty.

until one of us c
ould not stand it
any longer and
shot him.

La Tristesse

je suis triste
yes
sadder than sad
but i won't search
for another word
that one will suffice

je suis triste
my love is an empty
cradle that rocks
to and fro
without a sound
without a sound

without a sound

Dices

Dices
que eres de aquí
Pero
ni eres de aquí
ni de allá

Dices
que fuiste esto
Pero
nunca fuiste
na'

Y que
hiciste tal cosa
Pero
nunca se
realizó

'Fuera
de tu imaginación
Eres nomás—
el momento

Si eso no es
suficiente
ni existes—
en tu mente

Y
seguramente
ni en
la mía.

A November Verse

there is a little girl/una criatura/uma menina dôce
somewhere/por allí/não se
an Emily/una Alfonsina/uma Gabriela tal vez
and she will grow up/haciéndose vieja/morrer
never knowing/sin saber/sem viver

if i took her hand/acariciar su carita/falar com ela
and we flew away/dándole mi cariño/será a solução
maybe/tendría el ánimo/para seguir
she wouldn't be afraid/y llegaría mañana/para diante

From "A Letter to Alicia"

finally we are ending the cesspool
of the 20's
i remember you
you don't fool me
with your designer jeans
designer makeup
sculptured nails
and glittering teeth
we shared the same jar of noxema
i covered for you at the ruins of monte albán
while you changed your tampon
before the eyes of gods and ghosts
and scorpions
you tolerated my cigarette smoke
binges drinking alone into oblivion
finally we are no longer young
women men deposit their confusion
in leaving us with their memories
of past loves and their dirty underwear
we no longer cry into our poems our work
my man done gone and left me and before
we get to the last verse the ass is knock
ing on the door again (maybe he left
something important behind? surely he
couldn't have grown up overnight . . . ?)
finally we've come to respect our own
privacy slipping into quiet moments with
a cup of tea or glass of mellow wine re
flect on the next project and life is
balanced even new york seems to make sense
chicago is not quite as resistant as once

i think i remember saying back at 21
can't wait for these next ten years to pass
anticipating a lot of pain like a decade
of pure heartburn and gas . . .

Not Just Because My Husband Said

if i had no poems left
i would be classified *working class intelligentsia*
my husband said
having to resort to teaching or research
grow cobwebs between my ears
if i had no poems left

if i did not sing in the morning
or before i went to bed, i'd be as good as dead
my husband said
struck dumb with morose silence or apathy
my children would distrust me
if i did not sing in the morning

if i could not place on the table
fresh fruit, vegetables tender and green
we would soon grow ill and lean
my husband said
we'd grow weak and mean and useless to our neighbors
if i could not place fresh fruit on the table.

Seduction of the Poetess

Poems
along thighs
sweet nipples
like shriveled grapes
woven through
black hair . . .

Poems end there
in homage
of a ceremony
where clothing
is tossed
to the floor:

"Another glass
of wine, monsieur"
Yes, the lady wants
another glass. Is her
speech slurring yet;
is her face flushed?
Will she mind much if
I don't take her home?

"Another glass
of wine, monsieur . . . ?"
His grin reveals his
secret.

"Another glass of wine
monsieur, before i go . . .
because i *will*
put on my coat
place each button into
its hole, perfect balance
will have me at the door
leaving nothing
but one poem scrawled
on the bathroom wall.

Monsieur:
it is especially
for you. No other poems
will emanate from
this night.
Monsieur has sent
scurrying
soft rabbits in meadows
scurrying
huge grey rats in damp
basements.

Si acaso

. . . y si acaso
       hemos llegado
al fin del final
donde se termina
el camino
y te encuentras muy
       cansado
o nos encontramos
sin ánimo
para empezar
otro . . .
no te culpes
ni me culpo
ni debemos
       de pensarlo
¡Olvídalo!
Si acaso
       hemos llegado
a un espacio
roto
en el tejido
un sólo hilo
desenredándose
poco a poco
hasta que no
queda nada
sino la duda
del recuerdo . . .
Si acaso
       hemos llegado
a una fiesta

de disfraces
y no te conozco
ni tú a mí
bailaremos con
        sonrisas
de títeres
haciéndoles
        "ojos"
a los que nos
rodean
sonriéndonos
en un
        espejo.
Si acaso
        hemos llegado . . .

Cartas

Tus cartas
vienen
flotando
con pereza
como la hora
de siesta.
Me llegan
plumas tintas
de pájaros
engañosos.
Soñé anoche
íbamos las tres
(tú, ella, yo)
juntas
hasta que tormentas
aguas furiosas
sin necesidad
de amigas
nos hicieron presas
en una casa extraña
(tú, ella, yo)
tú
con el pelo de
maíz maduro
ella con labios
sangrientos
yo . . .

Guardo tus cartas
entre libros
sobre la mesa

en la cocina
manchadas de
manteca y café
llenas de polvo
quemadas del sol
heladas por inviernos
que nos unen
y se retiran
como ondas
de un mar jadesco.

Whole

i love juana
because she is not me
which is why i can
say her name
outright
unlike poets who hold
their most precious secrets
to silence

we are lovers of
life and reflection she
believes i'm better at
the latter while she is
best at the first so we
report with great enthu
siasm so as not to leave
anything out

we are children to
gether playing the Grand
Madames off to the theatre
the posh at brunch
the avant garde at the cinema
we dress up we strip down
sometimes we take our daughter
then we are two and a half
or three or a triangle
and whole

THE INVITATION

The Invitation

On a certain night
i will compose a verse:
                Long and Winding

                           from your mouth
                           to just below
                           the thighs

A rhyme of
quiet sunbursts
                Fingers

                           finding their way
                           to a subtle rhythm

On some afternoon
prose will become
                Movements

                           in perfect coordination
                           from hips to hips
                           lines will run along
                           the curve of your spine
                           on and on

Any day now
i will make you
a song
                Playfully Biting

                           a melody for dancing
                           when legs intertwine

Sometime very soon
my eyes will invite
you to create
                A Masterpiece

                           two bodies blending
                           into a poem
                           that never ends . . .

Dance of the Nebulae

His nostalgia
savored
  rich
    thick
black coffee
in a tiny porcelain
cup
  hot
    fine
grains of sand
chimes tinkling
in the Eastern
wind—

As he watched
her
  quietly
    sipping
red wine
  quietly
    stirring
blue fire
the music inspired
them to the
floor—

She waved
  invisible
    sheer
scarves

lured him to
         his
              knees
the teasing mole
on his chin praised
         her gyrating
              hips
he waved
         invisible
              shackles
key clenched
between her teeth—

Their movements
were the ripples
of the River Jordan
the sky
         wept
with thunderous
joy
         swept
their spirits
to an oasis
         of
              consummation
a void in time
where lovers
meet—
"Let us go lie
         between

a fold in the
night"
"Let us go!"
Each gesture
of the curving
    wrist
        called
each painted
    finger
        tip
the full contour
of his quivering
    lips
"Let us go"
pleaded their very
essence
    in
        vain—

So that the
    last
        mad
twirl
the sound of
    clapping
        hands
broke
the vibrant trance
and she
returned

quietly
       to sip
the red wine
as he watched
his nostalgia
     melt
       softly
into the yellow
walls.

Después de probar (la manzana)

¡Ay!
Que Cosita
      rica y sabrosa
      que entra y sale
      por la boca
      de mi río . . .
            con un ritmo
            que me vuelve
            loca—¡ay!

qué cosa
tan tremenda
madura y dulce
      gotea su jugo
      tropical—
      Después de probar
      la manzana . . .
            ¿que pensó Eva
            de esta curiosidad
            natural?

¿Qué importa
ahora que
tengo mi cosita
      antes de caer
      dormida a soñar
      de un jardín
      lleno . . .
            con matas
            de mangos
            ¡Qué buenos! ¡Ay!

Tierra del Fuego
(Dedicado a Gato Barbieri)

Tears bleed
through the pores
of your crying hom
as the beads
of sweat form
round your lips

Your finger twirling
painting rhythms
in the air

You kiss
the cool brass
to send blaring
firedrops
to dance
inside my skin

Burning deep
into my mind
until we are back
to another
place
to another
time . . . !

Gritos de pájaros locos
volando por el bosque
Cazadores negros
llenos de hambre . . .

Una voz llora
           resonando
           dejando

que el mundo sepa
del clímax que pasa
por su cuerpo . . .

¡Ay Madre!
¡Me Muero!
¡Gato-No te vayas!
Tú—que has llegado
con el cuerno que dejas
llorar para mí—iiiiiiiiiiiiiiiiiiiiiiiii!

Tango (de la luna)

En este tiempo
no sale el sol
o sale sin querer
sin querer
despierto
de un sueño
      al otro—

Entre media luz
saludo
a tu retrato
de ojos inmóviles
aún móviles
siguiéndome
de cuarto
      a cuarto—

Tu delgada boca
me llama
al cuadro donde
el tiempo
se ha
      ahogado—

Veo tu cuerpo
en miniatura
caderas anchas
la blusa
transparente
luce tus
      pezones—

Mi imagen
junto
a la tuya
llena de
jugos
            calientes—

Siento
el frío
del cristal
y el ardor
de tu
            aliento—

Se me
olvidó
tu nombre
cómo nos
conocimos
la fuente
al fondo
con agua
            congelada—

A la distancia
la luna
llama
al sol
que
            salga—

Pero no sale
el sol
el sol
no
      sale.

Coffee Break

15 minutes
> They take
> their morning papers
> monogrammed mugs
> to the lounge
> moaning and groaning
> of monday monotony
> & self boredom—

she

> does a 2 step down
> the narrow hall
> to the small room
> where toilet paper
> plugs the keyhole
> whitewashed windows
> graffitti wallpaper
> designed by unknown
> heroes and scholars—

A tiny streak

> of sun leaks
> through a space
> of unpainted glass
> makes as a spotlight
> for 2 talented fingers
> creating fast—
> > *ART IN MOTION!*
> >
> > *A STAR IS BORN!*
> >
> > *SUCH STYLE!*
> >
> > *WHAT GRACE!*

The cracked mirror
        reveals a winning face
        eternity stops just
        to applaud
        she takes a modest bow
        4½ minutes gone
        no time for an encore—

With a hum
        & a shuffle
        she returns to the bunch
        drinking stale coffee
        exchanging griefs &
        complaints

And
        she's singing
        "Isn't She Lovely"
        on her way
        to her desk
        thinking of lunch
        when she has
        30 FULL minutes:
        (the 2nd performance
        is always the best!)

What Only Lovers

Once
during our travels
when we stopped
in one of those hot
unbearable places
in one of those
nameless hotels

Once
after our fifth
shower
of that day
you stretched across
the hard bed
let your wet hair
hang over the headboard
and slept

i wanted to talk
to my companion
who was busy then
with a dream
at two
the afternoon was
thick liquid
i found myself
watching you
Once discovered
what only lovers
knew:
the slow rhythm

of your steady
breath
dark red nipples
standing erect
the black hair
on your legs
your legs
mountain climbing
legs
saturday night dancing
legs
legs for wrapping
Once
a roach rushed across
your still arm
and i envied it
my friend became
an ocean
and i wanted
to be taken
by each wave
Once the moon fell
on you
the stifling air
cooled against you
the whole room was
eden
taking a taste
of you . . .
and i wanted
to taste you
just once.

Otro Canto

talking proletariat talks
over instant coffee
and nicotine,
in better times
there is tea
to ease the mind
talking proletariat talks
during laid-off hours
cursing and cussing
complaining of unpaid bills
and bigoted unions
that refuse to let us in.

talking proletariat talks
of pregnant wives
and shoeless kids.
no-turkey-thanksgivings.
bare xmas tree this year.
santa claus is on strike
again.

talking proletariat talks
with proletariat friends
and relations who need
a few bucks 'til the end
of the week
waiting
for compensation checks.
talking proletariat talks
of plants closing down
and deportations.

tight immigration
busting our brothers again.

talking proletariat talks
of next spring or some
unforeseen vacation
to leave all this behind
to forget the winter
in unheated flats
turned off gas and
"ma bell" who serves
the people
took the phone away
when we were out
looking for a gig.

talking proletariat talks
of next presidential elections
the emperor of chicago
who lives off the fat of the land
and only feeds his sty of pigs.
talking proletariat talks
over rum and schlitz
of lottery tickets
on bingo nights at St. Sebastian's.

talking proletariat talks
climbing crime, defenseless
women, unsafe parks and
congested highways.
talking proletariat talks

of higher rent two months
behind, landlords who live
on lake shore drive or over
where the grass *is* greener.

talking proletariat talks
talking proletariat talks
talking proletariat talks
until one long
awaited day—
we are tired
of talking.

Milagros

Morenita clara
ojos grandes,
like those
          painted on
                    four for a dollar prints.
                    of shaggy pups
                    and ragged dolls—

hung up
     on the
                    bedroom walls
                    where her baby sleeps.

Milagros
talks about
the importance
of her education,
the state of affairs
on the island,
her husband—
who doesn't speak
English . . .
but that's okay.
They're going back home again anyway—
Someday
As she talks of these things,
you smile
     just to watch
          her beautiful face
                    shine

like her tropical sun:
Only a childhood memory
these days . . .
> When the ambition of a degree
> is taking the form of a dream . . .
> Another baby on the way,
> (Well, her husband never did like
> the idea of this college business
> anyway . . .)

These days are getting shorter.
The nights keep getting longer.
The kitchen clock starts ticking
> louder . . .

Milagros has no time to talk,
> her rice may overcook.

But just before
she turns away
you catch that look:
> painted on four for a dollar prints
> of shaggy pups and ragged dolls
> hung up on the bedroom walls

Where her
> baby
> > sleeps.

1974

El ser mujer . . .

I'm thinking of you. In the
silent hours of this infinite night
as I lay wrapped in the
protecting arms of my sleeping husband.
Querida Mami, am I not still
your "Cabellitos De Oro"
who once found her dreams
lying in the warmth of your bosom,
on those bleak and icy nights,
when the darkness became too great
for me to bear:

Mami, dime por favor, si puedes:
Must I be a woman now? I know
I bear the reflection of your youth.
Yet I am not ready to echo those
trying years. One by one
until the time comes when my
hands are filled with betraying
scars and wrinkles too.
Mami, I'm afraid!
I'm not as strong as you, yet,
I suppose there was a time
when you did not know your own
strength. You do now.
I'm thinking of you. In the
silent hours of this night.
I can hear your gentle voice whisper:

"Persígnate, mi hija." But it is to you—
I pray, Mi Querida Madre . . .
As my eyes surrender to the darkness.

                              1973

A Christmas Carol: c. 1976

Today i went downtown and signed away
another dream. i watched the other women
frown, the other women scream
with bitter sadness sign away their dreams;
as they became statistics for the
legal aid divorce division, new numbers
for the welfare line, eligible recipients
for social security benefits . . .
as they signed away.

Today i sat among them, with the
stoned face dignity necessary for one
who wears a borrowed coat for the winter cold;
and counts her change for the clark st. bus
while xmas shoppers push and shove,
among paperback readers/public sleepers:
i tuck away my dream into some distant past/
i tuck away a love that couldn't last,
but has. i stare at the appointment cards:
the court date/the job i hope to have,
but the only hope left is that winter won't last
forever/that winter won't last . . .
after all, nothing ever does:

A little girl held her mother's hand
with wide eyed fascination watched
the holiday decorations on state street/
the parade went by/santa claus with a crooked
cotton beard would wave/and mamá'd say:
"¿Ya ves? Pórtate bien y a ver qué te trae,"
and i wondered how santa claus would arrive

at a second floor flat in the back where even
those who lived on the block wouldn't go out
at night, but mamá went out each morning at
5 a.m. and on christmas day, a doll with pink
ribbons in its yellow hair and smelling of new
plastic, would always be there, 'cause after
all, i had been a good girl/i had always been
good.

Today i went downtown and walked
among the hurrying crowd, but no one
held my hand this time/no one smiled/
no one wished a merry xmas to anyone.
but i thought how nice it would be to buy
her something special this year/to send him
a greeting card/and how much nicer it would
be, to be a little girl again:

when dreams get tucked away in future spaces
instead, and my signature got nothing more
than a star in penmanship to take home and
paste proudly on a paint chipped wall:
"¿Ya ves que bien? A ver qué te trae Santa Claus,
a ver que te trae!" and that would be all.

Napa, California
(Dedicado al Sr. Chávez, sept. '75)

We pick
    the bittersweet grapes
    at harvest
    one
        by
            one
    with leather worn hands
                    as they pick
                        at our dignity
                        and wipe our pride
                        away
                        like the sweat we wipe
                        from our sun-beaten brows
                        at midday
In fields
    so vast
    that our youth seems
    to pass before us
    and we have grown
    very
        very
            old
                by dusk . . .
                (bueno pues, ¿qué vamos a hacer, Ambrosio?
                ¡bueno pues, seguirle, comprade, seguirle!
                ¡Ay, Mamá!
                Sí pues, ¿qué vamos a hacer, compadre?
                ¡Seguirle, Ambrosio, seguirle!)
We pick
    with a desire

that only survival
inspires
While the end
of each day only brings
a tired night
that waits for the sun
and the land
that in turn waits
for us . . .

A Counter-Revolutionary Proposition

Let's forget
that Everything matters
for awhile: beneath
the covers
we'll block out the
afternoon sun, icicled
windows; a pile of bills
instead of Christmas cards;
Christians and Jews, land
reform news, another old
lady beat to death in a cold
water flat; a friend who needs
a fix, big time dealer taking
a sip from a coconut out
in the Bahamas; Mamá and menopause;
another leak in the basement:

Let's forget
all this
for just awhile and make
a little love . . .
and make a little love,
instead.

Strategy

you are there
waiting in a field
of chaos
blood and steel
building walls
between us

i am here
waiting like the sun
patiently allowing the night
and its threats
of mysterious infinity
to pass

but you and i
are destined
to join
a soldier of light
a soldier of strength

do not fear
this timeless phase
for the rays of this sun
will melt the steel
and dry the blood

upon the land
that will once again
be ours.

FIVE RANDOM ARROWS

1974–1982

Juego

Allí esta el dolor
otro recuerdo frágil
no debes tocar

No se ve
no busques en los ojos
u otras partes famosas
por su chisme

En un espacio no más
grande que una peseta
se juntó todo el cuento

¿Ves? Allí está tu nombre
grabado pequeño pero sin
duda tuyo

Hay fechas menos claras
hechos y eventos históricos
que no se encontrarán
en otro calendario

Con importancia dada sólo
por mi terco romanticismo

(¿No te dije que no toques?
¿qué voy a hacer contigo?)

1982

La una y cuarto

¿Es posible que las horas pasarán más lentas?
Estirándose como elástico y fallando la ley
natural,

¿Es posible aguantar horas tan hondas y vacías?
Ollas inmensas de barro negro, frágil y corriente.

¡Me haré vieja sin que pase un día y es peor
la noche! Un viaje entero sin destino antes
de amanecer.

¡Dame un martillo para quebrar la cara cínica
del reloj con sus brazos cruzados, sacándome
la lengua!

¡Voy a poner una bomba en la cómpañía de teléfono
porque el mío no suena y no pagaré mi cuenta
tampoco!

Le voy a quejar a dios, escribirle al gobernador
deshacerme del presidente. Al cabo ni voté por el.

1982

Last Sunday

Your best friend is dying.
The medical experts have set a date.
They did the best they could.
(Isn't that what they always say
when the "best" hasn't been good enough?)
God damn! I mean . . .
they cut the man up!
What the . . . !

While you were tossing big plans
around in your heads,
(the pressures of turning thirty);
Butch always having been so quick
with making things work. You
couldn't lose! Suddenly . . .
what kind of trick is this?
I mean . . .

No, no. Calm down. He needs you now.
Don't be so cynical.
(It gets so redundant cursing fate out
time after time.)
It hasn't been all bad.
Just the other night you both joked
about the past, growing up.
Nothing ever got him down.
Nothing was ever that bad . . .

There's something you have to tell him now.
It came to you sometime during these last
three sleepless nights, since you got

the news from his wife. What was it?
It couldn't have been anything romantic
or philosophical. All of it surely
having gone through his mind already,
with much more clarity. (The way it only
can to a man who knows his designated hour.)

Was it something he left behind
when he came by to shoot the breeze,
smoke a joint? (The doctors had already
forbidden him to drink.) You look
around frantically—for a glove,
a set of keys. You were here, Butch,
weren't you? You had to leave something
behind!

You can't leave just like that, man!
Cut and dry. Like some statistic.
The 999,999th Puerto Rican born
in the state of New York in 1949.
Didn't we talk about this?
Taking control of the circumstances.
No more dirty spics, half nigger,
half white; we were gonna do it right!
Ride high! Do it right and ride high
a long time!

Wait a minute. Control.
Think now. Maybe you wrote it down,
in the journal you've picked up
since all of a sudden it seems

important to document today,
that becomes yesterday, just like that,
then last week, last month, last
winter, last year . . . !
Now I remember, Butch! I remember.
But it's stuck here, between my thumping heart
and tied up throat. I remember.
I love you, man.
I love you, my brother.

1979

Invierno salvaje

Invierno salvaje—
¿Intentas matarnos?
No tendrás
el honor.
Las fábricas
nos esperan
y la voz
del mayordomo
es aún más fuerte
que la tuya.
Las oficinas
de la Torre Sears
Los Steel Mills
y la multitud
de tiendas y restaurantes
nos llaman,
día tras día, noche tras noche.
La hambre que sentimos antes
nos obliga a trabajar.
Somos las maquinitas
que brillan los pisos
de los hospitales
y cada vidrio del John Hancock.

Crees que tu mordida—
brava como sea—
y que congela los pies
y a las manos azulea
nos cortará el circuito?

No, invierno salvaje. No.

Aunque recordamos esa tierra
con sol constante, playas blancas,
y las palmas que bailaban en la brisa—
son lujos de turistas, los políticos,
el presidente de la compañía.
Nada más que un recuerdo
para los demás. Así que te suplico,
de parte de cada uno—¡vete ya!
Y deja de burlarte.
Que nos llama algo más grande
y amenazante: nos llama la vida.

Winter 1975, más o menos

Our Tongue Was Nahuatl

You.
We have never met
yet
we know each other
well.
i recognized
your high
        set
            cheekbones,
slightly rounded
           nose,
the deep brown of your hardened
face, soft
full lips.

Your near-slanted eyes
follow me—
sending flashback memories
to your so-called
primitive mind.
And i know
you remember . . .

It was a time
of turquoise blue green,
sky topped mountains,
god-suns, wind-swept rains;
oceanic deities
naked children running
in the humid air.

i ground corn
upon a slab of stone
while you bargained
at the market
dried skins
and other things
that were our own.

i watched our small sons
chase behind your bare legs
when you came home those days.
We sat, ate,
gave thanks to our golden Earth.
Our tongue was Nahuatl.
We were content—
with the generosity
of our gods and our kings,
knowing nothing of the world
across the bitter waters—
Until they came . . .

White foreign strangers
riding high
                on four-legged
                creatures;
that made us bow to them.
In our ignorance of the unknown
they made us bow.

They made us bow—
until our skin became
the color of caramel
and nothing anymore
was our own.

Raped of ourselves,
our civilization,
even our gods turned away
from us in shame . . .

Yet we bowed,
                as we do now—

On buses
                going to factories
where "No Help Wanted" signs
laugh at our faces,
stare at our hungry eyes.

Yet we bow . . .
                WE BOW!
It was a time
much different
                than now.

Chicago, 1974